Leading Virtual Teams

Pocket Mentor Series

The *Pocket Mentor* Series offers immediate solutions to common challenges managers face on the job every day. Each book in the series is packed with handy tools, self-tests, and real-life examples to help you identify your strengths and weaknesses and hone critical skills. Whether you're at your desk, in a meeting, or on the road, these portable guides enable you to tackle the daily demands of your work with greater speed, savvy, and effectiveness.

Books in the series:

Leading
Virtual
Teams

Expert
Solutions to
Everyday Challenges

Harvard Business Press

Boston, Massachusetts

Library of Congress Cataloging-in-Publication Data

Leading virtual teams : expert solutions to everyday challenges.
     p. cm. — (Pocket mentor series)
  Includes bibliographical references.
  ISBN 978-1-4221-2886-2 (pbk. : alk. paper)
 1. Virtual work teams—Management.
  HD66.L438 2009
  658.4'022—dc22

                           2009005482

Contents

Keeping Team Members Aligned Through Communication 25

Tips for maintaining open lines of communication.

Using Coaching to Enhance Team Performance 35

Ideas for using coaching to ensure high performance from your team.

Leveraging Technology Effectively 41

Suggestions for getting the most value from communication and meeting technology.

Tips and Tools

Mentors' Message:
The Power
of Virtual Teams

In this age of globalization and advances in communication technology, it's more common than ever for companies to have virtual teams—teams in which some or all members are working in different geographic locations. Virtual teams provide unique advantages for an organization as well as raise special kinds of challenges that their leaders must address.

If you've been charged with leading a virtual team for the first time, get ready for an interesting and challenging—as well as satisfying—experience! You'll need to augment your usual managerial skills with new ones designed specifically for this type of team.

In this guide, you'll find a wealth of suggestions for getting the most value from your virtual team, as well as tools and tactics you can put to work immediately while assembling your team and guiding its progress. Leading a virtual team can be difficult in some ways, but it's also rewarding. By mastering this managerial skill, you can make a major contribution to your organization.

Jessica Lipnack and Jeffrey Stamps, Mentors

Jessica Lipnack and Jeffrey Stamps are CEO and Chief Scientist, respectively, of the Boston-based consulting firm NetAge (www. netage.com) and authors of many books and articles on networked organizations, including *Virtual Teams* (New York: John Wiley & Sons, Inc., 2000).

Leading
Virtual
Teams:
The Basics

Why Virtual Teams?

As a manager, you probably hear a lot about virtual teams these days. Maybe you've led one or more of them. With technology making it easier than ever for far-flung employees to work together, it's no surprise that virtual teams are becoming more common. In the following sections, we explore what virtual teams are, why they're valuable, and what challenges they present for managers seeking to lead them.

What are virtual teams?

The term *virtual team* refers to a team that, for the most part, is linked through communication—for example, through e-mail, voice mail, telephone, videoconferencing, and Internet-based forums—rather than face-to-face. Many of today's teams are virtual to some extent—that is, they include members who are physically separated from their teammates or come together from different organizations. These may be company employees who work in different global locations, representatives of a key supplier, or perhaps even important customers. Some teams are entirely virtual; their members rarely, if ever, meet face-to-face. Nevertheless, virtual teams are real teams, and when they perform their missions well, they offer numerous advantages to companies.

Why are virtual teams valuable?

Virtual teams provide a number of different forms of value for organizations. For example, they often operate on a twenty-four-hour cycle. With virtual teams working literally around the world, a company can stay open twenty-four-hours a day. At quitting time in Hamburg, the German members of a virtual team can forward the result of their day's work to their U.S. colleagues based in New York. Those team members will begin their day where their German colleagues left off, eventually forwarding the output of their day's work to another group in Sydney, Australia. Like relay racers, these team members keep the baton, or work, moving forward, around the clock.

Virtual teams also tap the strength of diversity. They make it easier for organizations to bring together an extremely diverse group of people with varying skills, experiences, and knowledge about customers and business.

Consider this example: a team of product developers is working on a new electronic household appliance aimed at a worldwide market. By design, its team members are based in North America, Europe, and Asia and are native to those regions. This arrangement strengthens the team's ability to recognize customer tastes and product use and to incorporate the safety and electrical standards of different countries.

Thanks to the cultural diversity represented on this virtual team, the team stands a much better chance of developing a successful product. That achievement might not have been possible if the product had been developed by a team located in a single research and development facility.

*This market-creating or virtual prototyping piece of our business
allows the customer to have what he wants very rapidly . . .
Essentially, we are creating products the customer wants virtually
at his doorstep, much like one would order a pizza.*
  —David Ross

What challenges do virtual teams bring?

The principles that govern a virtual team are essentially the same
as those for a team managed in one location. Managers of virtual
teams must ensure clarity of goals, bring together the right set
of skills, gain member commitment, and so forth. They must also
encourage adequate collaboration and information sharing and
create rewards that align effort with team goals.

But there's something different about *virtual* work, and leaders
of virtual teams face some unique challenges. Specifically, such
teams present *management* challenges: their leaders must figure
out how to apply what they know about managing teams to coordi-
nating virtual work. These teams also pose *technological* challenges:
leaders must ask themselves which tools will best enable them to
keep members connected, communicating, and collaborating.

*Virtual teams are live, not Memorex. They are most definitely
teams, not electronic versions of the real thing.*
  —Jessica Lipnack and Jeffrey Stamps

In the sections that follow, we explore various aspects of these
challenges in more detail and lay out some ideas for surmounting
them.

Setting the Stage for Success in Your Virtual Team

As with any team, getting the most value from your virtual team requires establishing a firm foundation for success. That foundation includes clarity on goals, roles, and processes; clear definition of leadership responsibilities; and the right type of team culture. Let's look at each of these more closely.

Achieving clarity on goals, roles, and processes

All teams need clearly defined visions and *goals*. For example, a virtual team's goal might be to develop a new product, devise a strategy for entering a new market, or propose a new information technology (IT) system after analyzing a set of alternatives.

However, a virtual team may find it harder to achieve clarity about goals than a same-place team does. After all, competent members of a same-place team may easily clarify a vague vision, adjust poorly defined goals, and transform an ill-defined project into a realistic one just by being near one another. They can readily talk in the halls, at lunch, and in the parking lot to straighten out problems or misunderstandings.

Virtual teams simply don't have that luxury. Like any other team, a virtual one will examine and adjust its goals during the work process. However, its leader and members should also map out the clearest possible vision and overall goals at the beginning if they hope to achieve their objective. The goals need to be concrete and measurable (for example, "Complete a prototype of the new product by the end of the year"). That way, at the end of the effort, the team can look back and know that it has achieved the desired results.

As with team vision and goals, the *roles* of virtual team members must be clearly defined from the beginning. For instance, who is going to conduct market research for the proposed new product? Who will handle development of the product prototype? Who will decide what form the prototype will take (for example, a computer simulation or a physical prototype)? Without clarity about roles, team members can get bogged down in confusion and can end up duplicating one another's efforts or even working at cross-purposes.

Early agreement about individual roles can also help ensure that virtual team members not only take responsibility for separate tasks but also view their work as part of the big picture. Working together, members can see what needs to be done and make sure that someone is there to do it.

The speed at which you can communicate defines how quickly you can make money. If I can respond to a customer in six hours anywhere in the world at any time, that's a competitive advantage.
—Bob Buckman

Finally, the virtual workplace requires explicit, transparent *processes* (decision-making approaches, methodologies, work plans, procedures) and *outputs* (deliverables, records, milestones, results, documents). To illustrate the need for clarity of processes, will the team use "majority rule" or "complete consensus" to make decisions? What procedures will members use to update one another on their work? As an example of clarity in outputs, what milestones

What Would YOU Do?

Going to the Dogs?

TOM IS EXCITED. A manager in the product development department at a large sporting-goods company, he has been chosen to lead an experienced, talented, and highly skilled team that will develop a new type of training collar for hunting dogs. But he's also nervous. Members of the team are scattered around the globe in different cities, cultures, and time zones. Tom wonders how the team will communicate with each other when some members are asleep and others are awake. Also, will the members be able to collaborate well even though they come from such different cultures and backgrounds? And how will they keep track of ongoing work?

This impressive array of talent has the promise of great success. Yet Tom knows that working virtually can also hobble teams. He once worked on a virtual team, and the project fell apart after some members failed to inform other members about problems they had encountered in their own parts of the effort. Tom wonders how he can set the stage for success for *his* team.

What would YOU do? The mentors will suggest a solution in *What You COULD Do.*

must the team achieve, and by when, in order to deliver on its agreed-upon goals?

Transparency in these areas means that all team members understand and agree on the processes and desired outputs. It also enables the team to produce consistent results: everyone on the team knows what the team is trying to achieve—and how the team is going to achieve it.

Clarity on all these fronts encourages commitment to the team and its goals, and that's critical for any team's success. People commit to things that they see as very important—either important projects or achievements crucial to their careers. If team members lack commitment, they will allocate their energy and time to other goals and will participate in the team only to the extent that their schedules permit.

The most practical way to obtain commitment within a virtual team is to be very selective about whom you invite to join it. Within the constraint of required skills, leaders should pick people who have strong, natural interests in the team's goals. "Steps for Assembling a Virtual Team" provides additional suggestions for how to put your team together.

Defining leadership responsibilities

In addition to clarity about goals, roles, and processes, virtual teams need clarity about leadership responsibilities. The very reason for a virtual team's existence may be to pull together people with special expertise and experience who do not work together in the same geographic space. As on any team in which many highly

Steps for Assembling a Virtual Team

So, you've determined that you need to assemble a virtual team to address a specific purpose. Where do you start? The following steps can help:

1. **Define the purpose.** The best predictor of a virtual team's success is the clarity of its purpose and the participatory process by which the group achieves it. Work with team members to define the purpose of your team in clear, compelling language. For example, "Our purpose is to create a Web site that will accommodate e-commerce for all three product lines, make site updating and expansion faster and less costly, and enhance our customers' experience." Make sure everyone interprets the purpose statement in the same way and agrees on it.

2. **Identify needed skills and personal qualities.** Ask yourself what skills, knowledge, and expertise will be essential to the team's success. Look beyond technical abilities to include problem-solving talents, capacity to work effectively with others, and understanding of the company's political and logistical landscape. Consider ability to master new skills as needed and capacity to exchange information, write well, and speak clearly and comfortably on the telephone. In addition, you'll need team members who have the following personal qualities:

   - They are highly self-disciplined and motivated. These team members will be responsible for staying on schedule and asking for help when necessary. A virtual team is not ideal for people who need a great deal of supervision.

- They are open-minded to new technology. Members may need to learn new, fairly simple technology that will help everyone on the team connect and communicate with one another.

3. **Identify people with the required skills and qualities.** Look within *and* outside your organization to find people who have the required skills and qualities you've identified. Consider peers, direct reports, suppliers, customers, and consultants. Contact respected colleagues to ask for their opinions about who might make valuable members of the team.

4. **Choose your virtual team.** Consider the following processes for selecting team members:
   - Invite them to join your virtual team.
   - Ask people to volunteer.
   - Ask people who have an interest in the project to nominate individuals who have the right skills and qualities.

---

competent people are brought together, leadership should be shared—because no one member has all the answers.

On a virtual team, leadership typically shifts depending on the task at hand. As a team leader, you too should be willing to share the amount of direction and control that you exert over a project. Likewise, team members should be willing to offer their guidance and managerial expertise as needed.

For example, suppose a virtual team has been charged with developing a new consumer product. How might team members share leadership? In this case, the member of the team who has the most technical expertise might take responsibility for evaluating and selecting the electronic components for the product. Meanwhile, the team member with the greatest knowledge of customer needs might make decisions about product features. A member with marketing expertise may shoulder responsibility for communicating the product's benefits in advertising campaigns. Likewise, if an unexpected conflict with a supplier over component pricing crops up, the team member with the strongest negotiation skills might take charge of resolving that conflict.

Assessing the team's culture

If members of a virtual team are global or new to the group, it's useful to do a "culture check" to ensure that members have the right attitudes, behaviors, and values to make the team successful. Consider asking team members how they feel about the following:

- **Working conditions:** How much will team members be expected to travel? What resources will be available to them for getting their work done?

- **Hours of operation:** How many hours per day or week are team members expected to work? How early or late are team members expected to be available for phone conferences? For example, if the virtual team you're leading has a member in Taiwan and one in Germany, when can the team confer by phone so that some members aren't participating in phone conferences in the middle of the night (their time)? Expectations about work during weekends, holidays, or overtime may also vary. As the team leader, you need to carefully

What You COULD Do

Remember Tom's concern about how to set the stage for success in the virtual team he'll be leading?

Here's what the mentors suggest:

Tom can liken his role to that of a sports coach—guiding his virtual team toward a common goal. Many of the tasks Tom needs to complete for a virtual team are similar to those he would perform when leading any team. But when a team is working virtually, the chances of things going wrong are much greater. First, Tom and his team should establish a clear vision and workable goals. Then they should work together to define roles and responsibilities as well as to establish explicit work processes. Tom should think about doing a "culture check," engaging the team to establish operating agreements in regard to working conditions, hours, authority, delegation, communications, and other culturally determined activities. As a team, they should agree on ways for people to connect regularly, such as a weekly conference call or Internet chat, to help the team build a virtual community. This will pave the way for the best possible working relations during the project.

consider these questions, encourage team members to clarify expectations, and work out ways for people to share the burden of working at nonstandard times.

- **Authority and delegation:** Who will be responsible for making what types of decisions as the team does its work? Who has the authority to assign work to specific team members?

- **Communication patterns:** What are team members' assumptions about appropriate and acceptable communication—in particular, what is considered polite or impolite communication? For instance, in some countries, a manager who does not maintain a proper distance and sharply defined role in his or her working relationships with subordinates loses respect. In such cultures, managers may not welcome shared decision making.

By clarifying these issues before starting its work and revisiting them as problems arise, a virtual team can avoid misunderstandings and resentments later.

Fostering Team Identity

Individuals who identify with a team exhibit behaviors that form the bedrock of team success. They work harder, collaborate more, and, in many cases, put the team's interests ahead of their own. Identifying with a group usually goes hand in hand with trust, which in turn encourages information sharing and collaboration.

Team identity doesn't necessarily happen automatically in virtual teams, for obvious reasons. If the team and its members are out of sight, they also can be out of mind. In the worst cases, the virtual team is a collection of strangers with few, if any, social bonds. Although it's difficult to develop a sense of identity with a group of people whom you seldom, if ever, see, leaders of virtual teams *can* take steps to strengthen team identity. Holding a launch meeting, establishing operating agreements, communicating frequently using a variety of media, and encouraging collaboration can help.

Holding a launch meeting

If possible, gather all members of your virtual team together for a face-to-face project launch meeting—even if it's the only time that team members can convene during the course of the team's work. Devote one or two days to this meeting. While the group is together, create opportunities for members to get acquainted on a personal level. The goal is to create small-group cohesion. For example, introduce each member and ask him or her to say something about his or her background, special skills, hobbies, personal interests, and so forth.

Over the course of the one- or two-day launch meeting, assign people to subgroups, each charged with discussing a particular facet of the task. Rotate people in these subgroups so that everyone gets a chance to meet and work with everyone else. At the end of the launch meeting, take a group picture, send copies to all participants, and post it to the team Web site.

Establishing communication protocols

Set up ways for members of your team to talk together and communicate regularly. Here are some ideas.

- **Encourage periodic face-to-face meetings as the work progresses.** If the team is not too broadly dispersed—and if the budget permits—bring people together again at key junctures (for example, after several new members have joined the team, when key decisions must be made, or when the next phase of the project must be planned and assigned). Use videoconferencing if physical meetings are not feasible and the group is reasonably small. Doing so will reinforce the group bonding that occurred at the team launch. If you cannot bring the entire team together, do so for important subgroups.

- **Find times when people can get together on the phone.** This is bound to be difficult for teams that span continents and time zones, so schedule regular meeting times for conference calls or online discussions, and arrange a process for bringing up concerns about the project. This will help team members feel comfortable about sharing comments and will promote a team approach instead of encouraging people to work individually.

One warning: if the organization's headquarters is in the United States, don't schedule conference calls or Internet chats so that the Asian or Australian team members must always take calls or be online during regular U.S. business hours, which would be in the middle of the night for them. Doing so will annoy your partners on the other side of the globe. Instead, alternate conference call or Internet chat times so that any time-zone inconvenience is shared equally.

- **Reiterate the team's common goals.** Frequently revisit the team's shared goals and purpose to remind people that the work they are doing is important not just to the team, but to the organization as well.

"Steps for Communicating with a Virtual Team" and "Tips for Selecting Communication Media" offer additional suggestions.

Encouraging collaboration

The point of any team is to get people with complementary capabilities to work *together* on important tasks. But is collaboration possible among *virtual* team members? The answer is yes— collaboration is not only possible, but also can be strengthened and, when done properly, create results that not only equal but

Steps for Communicating with a Virtual Team

1. **Start with a face-to-face project launch meeting.** If possible, bring everyone together for a face-to-face project launch meeting. Virtual teams that begin this way hit the ground running. Even if everyone can't be in the same location, try to get as many people together as possible. Include off-site members by conferencing them in by phone or video. But don't despair if you can't meet face-to-face! You can do a lot in a series of ninety-minute conference calls to get things off on the right foot.

2. **Establish communication guidelines.** As with any team, a virtual team must create guidelines about when to communicate, what to communicate about, and how to communicate. Decide how the team will "meet" on a regular basis—phone conferences, videoconferences, face-to-face gatherings. Obviously, not everyone must be present at every meeting.

3. **Agree on standards and protocols for communicating.** Determine who will receive what types of communication and when. Who will be copied on what? Determine how frequently people will check e-mail and voice mail, and how promptly they will be expected to respond to such messages.

4. **Work out ways to communicate spontaneously.** Same-place teams have the opportunity to converse spontaneously— whether it's in the lunchroom, the hallway, or someone's office. Because virtual teams are typically dispersed, they lack this spontaneity. Although it's an oxymoron, "planned spontaneity" can actually work. Regular phone conversations and even an

open chat area on a Web site enable people to continue sharing ideas and working together.

5. **Document expectations about processes and results.**
Although agreeing on processes and results is important, it's equally critical to document what's been decided. This document may take the form of a written work plan or team charter that's made available on a team Web site (and e-mailed if necessary). The goal is to ensure that the same information is accessible to every team member—and that everyone is on the same page with what has been decided.

---

also outperform face-to-face teams. Here are some strategies for encouraging collaboration in your virtual team:

- **Promote collaborative work.** Find as many opportunities as possible to get people working together. For example, encourage several team members to solve an unexpected problem that has cropped up. Or ask a subgroup of team members to evaluate potential new suppliers for a product component and select the best one.

- **Recognize and praise collaborative behavior when you see it.** As the team's work progresses, watch for accomplishments that enable the team to excel, and communicate your appreciation to members. To illustrate, if several members collaborated successfully to solve a problem, send an e-mail to all team members expressing your appreciation and explaining how the achievement helped the team overall. Then, on the team conference call, recognize them again. If possible,

Tips for Selecting Communication Media

- How important is your message? Important messages should be easy to save and refer back to. E-mails, documents, and faxes can become permanent records.

- How complicated is it? If you can say it in a sentence or two, e-mail or voice mail is fine. If it's fairly long and complicated, consider attaching a file to an e-mail, sending a fax, or talking to someone on the phone. Ideally, everything should be posted to the team's Web site, which ensures that everyone has access to the same version of the same information.

- What do you need to know? If you need feedback from several people, consider asking for a phone conference. If input does not have to be simultaneous, a discussion among the key participants on the team's Web site may work. E-mail is always a fallback.

- How urgent is it? Some people rarely check e-mail; some are unreachable by phone but listen to voice mail; some read messages on their PDAs while moving around during the day and respond at night. Know the habits of your team members, and communicate in a way that will work for them.

- What will be the emotional impact? If the recipient is likely to have a strong reaction to the message (good or bad), send it in a more personal format. Remember that the phone remains a great way to communicate.

- If you're responding to a message, you don't always have to respond in the same medium.

- Written media (posting to the team Web site, attachments to e-mail) are best for detailed, complex messages or when you or the recipient will need a permanent record.
- Voice media (phone, voice mail, teleconference) are best for urgent messages, or when collaboration and conversation are important.

---

reward truly great team achievements with small tokens of appreciation. Your goal is to foster the feeling that team members are dependent on one another to achieve success—and that each member brings vital, complementary skills and knowledge to the effort.

- **Reiterate the team's value.** Frequently remind team members why their project matters to the organization. For example, will the new product they're developing raise revenues? Will the new market they're analyzing boost profitability and market share? When people can see how their efforts will pay off for the team and the company, they'll be more likely to work together to fulfill their mission.

Keeping Team Members Aligned Through Communication

As we've noted, members of a virtual team don't have access to coffee-room conversations or opportunities to detect distress signals through one another's body language and gestures. For this reason, it's important to create open lines of communication to ensure that team members easily send messages to one another and remain aligned behind the goal. These open lines of communication enable team members to establish mutual trust—perhaps the most vital ingredient in any high-performing team's ability to succeed.

The following communication practices can help you keep team members aligned.

Sustaining agreement about processes and results

Ensuring that everyone on a virtual team understands processes and desired results requires thoughtful discussion and ongoing updates. As your team begins its work, periodically check in with members to gauge their agreement on the questions you explored earlier, as well as additional ones important to moving the team's work forward. Specifically, explore these questions:

- What exactly is the team setting out to accomplish?

- When must we accomplish it?

- How will we make decisions?

- Who is responsible and accountable for the different parts of the project?

- How will we achieve our goals?

- How will we know when we have finished our work?

- How will we monitor progress and performance?

- How will we measure our results?

Great discoveries and improvements invariably involve
the cooperation of many minds.
—Alexander Graham Bell

Documenting expectations

Although agreeing on processes and results is important, managers also need to document what's been decided as their teams work to carry out their purpose. This document may take the form of a regularly updated written work plan or team charter that's posted to the team Web site or e-mailed to all team members, if necessary. By posting versions to the Web site, the team members avoid working on the wrong draft. Another useful document is an up-to-date team roster—a list of all team members, their roles on the team, the best way to contact them, their location and time zone, and the hours during which they are available for participating in phone conferences or videoconferences and responding to e-mails. This too should be posted to the team's Web site.

The key is to ensure that the information is accurate and accessible to every team member throughout the team's work—and that

?

What Would YOU Do?

The Trouble with Expectations

Sheila is a project manager for London-based Timmins Engineering, a specialized engineering development company with a niche market in measurement devices and with clients around the world. Whenever the company wins a new contract, it forms a virtual team to carry out the work. A team typically consists of the following people: professionals from Timmins, most of whom telecommute; independent consultants and technical specialists from many countries; and project managers from the client company.

Recently, OMD, a Shanghai-based firm, hired Timmins Engineering to help it develop a highly complex measurement device—on a tight schedule and limited budget. To produce the device on time, Sheila's group will need to work like a championship relay team. She assembles the team and then thinks about setting expectations about how the group will work together.

She wonders which expectations, exactly, she should focus on. To accommodate the tight deadline and different time zones, should she ask people to be available for phone conferencing during occasional evenings and weekends? Would it be better to focus on building a sense of community—for example, by encouraging people to chat informally and socially by e-mail or phone when such opportunities arise? What about leveraging each team member's unique expertise—should she clarify expectations about how different members' roles might need to shift depending on the task at hand? Should she ask the team itself to resolve these issues?

What would YOU do? The mentors will suggest a solution in *What You COULD Do.*

---

everyone is on the same page with what has been decided. "Steps for Creating a Work Plan" offers additional recommendations.

Keeping everyone informed

You and your team have established procedures for keeping everyone updated on what has been accomplished and which decisions have been made as the team's work progresses. The challenge is to ensure that team members communicate progress on their parts of the project—and ask for help from others as needed—and that the resulting information and updates circulate easily among all team members.

Leaders of virtual teams should encourage their teams to mutually decide who will submit what kinds of information to whom, and how often they will do it. The leader's job is to make sure these exchanges transpire so that things are happening as planned. For example, are team members updating their progress, as agreed? Do you or someone else on the team need to take responsibility for contacting team members to gather such information? Settle on a method, make any changes needed, and stick to agreed-upon methods so that everyone knows what to expect.

Steps for Creating a Work Plan

1. **Create a shared online workspace.** The work plan is your touchstone. It directs team and individual efforts and lets members hold one another accountable for getting the work done. Work plans are important anywhere, but in the virtual workspace they are crucial. Select easy-to-use software to create and post your work plan. See what conferencing and document-management software is available in your company—and use it. Many companies have systems that include calendars, schedules, discussions, and decision tracking.

2. **Agree on the contents of the plan.** Create the work plan together. Make sure the plan contains all the information each team member will need to do the work. Add elements as needed and use the current project's amended work plan as the basis for the next project's work plan. Post your work plan on the team Web site.

3. **Assign a team member as "keeper" of the plan.** Select one team member to serve as the first "keeper" of the work plan. But then rotate the job so all members learn how to maintain the plan, and no one person gets burdened with it. It's essential for everyone to understand how important—and how difficult—it is to keep the plan updated.

4. **Monitor the plan.** Keep your work plan accurate, up-to-date, and always accessible to team members. Encourage the entire team to take responsibility for monitoring the plan and alerting others to needed changes.

5. **Update the plan as needed.** Remind team members that any changes made to the work plan will affect other tasks and team members' work.

6. **Communicate changes made to the plan.** When the work plan changes, people must receive notification. Most team software includes this capability so that notification of changes is automatic. The keeper's job is to make sure everyone is tracking the notifications.

Also make sure that everyone has easy access to updates. You can do this through several means. For instance:

- Post weekly lists to the team Web site indicating which decisions have been made and what their status is (for example, "We've selected the vendor for the XYZ component, and Kuan is going to negotiate the contract. We still need to decide how to fix the low-voltage problem on the instrument. Paolo, Rana, and Gerta will discuss this week and propose a solution."). Use e-mail as backup, if necessary.

- Use the team's weekly meetings—either via conference call or videoconference, if available—to assess the effectiveness of the team's processes and to make any needed procedural changes.

- Post team progress reports and the status of decisions to the team Web site, and encourage all team members to consult the site daily to stay current.

What You COULD Do

Remember Sheila's worries about how to clarify expectations after assembling her virtual team?

Here's what the mentors suggest:

Sheila should focus her effort on getting the team to collaboratively clarify expectations regarding shared leadership on her team. Many virtual teams include people with specialized expertise who work in different physical places. No single member has all the answers. Sheila and each team member should be willing to share leadership or hand off leadership responsibility to one another depending on the task at hand and the stage of the project. For example, during the early project-planning stages, perhaps OMD's project manager in Shanghai should take primary responsibility for leading virtual meetings and monitoring early goal progress. Later, during the design stage, leadership could shift to Timmins Engineering's design specialist at its London headquarters.

Rather than laying out expectations about being available for phone conferencing, Sheila should first do a "culture check" to ask members to agree on shared views of working conditions, hours, and communication patterns. For example, in some cultures, workers are never expected to be available during weekends or holidays, or to put in overtime.

Sheila should also be careful about encouraging informal, social chitchat among team members. In this multicultural team, members may have different attitudes about working relationships. For example, in some countries, professionals consider social chatter or informal conversations about family and personal life inappropriate in a working relationship. Only after the whole team familiarizes itself with one another's various cultural attitudes should they agree to community-building procedures that are acceptable and comfortable for everyone.

Be consistent and reliable in ensuring that information flows fluidly. That way, team members know what to expect and can rely on getting the information they need—when they need it.

Using Coaching to Enhance Team Performance

In a team whose members are located in one place, the team leader can usually improve performance through coaching. For example, the following situations might require coaching:

- One team member doesn't know how to work with others.

- Another member must develop a presentation but has never used the technical software needed to generate the underlying data.

- Yet another member is having trouble developing a budget report.

In each of these instances, the team leader should coach the person needing assistance.

A virtual team has similar opportunities and needs for coaching, but getting the job done is more difficult. With members scattered in different locations and different time zones, the communication required for effective coaching is less available. A virtual team leader cannot simply walk over to the other person's office and demonstrate how to use the technical software or how to set up a budget report. Instead, he or she must make a special effort to provide the needed coaching. If you're in this situation, you can strengthen your ability to provide coaching by facilitating communication, clarifying priorities, easing any isolation team members may be experiencing, and addressing performance problems.

Facilitating communication

Here are some tips for encouraging the easy communication you need to coach.

- **Maintain strong lines of communication.** Keep lines of communication open so that team members know what's going on and what problems need addressing to move the team's work forward. For example, consider daily conference calls during crunch periods.

- **Encourage team members to help one another.** Make sure members of the team know about one another's unique skills and knowledge. Suggest that they call on one another for coaching assistance if needed.

- **Set intersecting office hours.** Flexible hours are a big advantage of virtual work. But too much flexibility can make it hard for team leaders to reach members who need coaching or for members to coach one another. Designate intersecting times of "virtual co-location" when all members can be reached, and make sure people know when it's okay to call one another. Work out compromises for different time zones and sleep habits. Make a rule to respect agreed-upon hours for communication.

Clarifying priorities

To coach members of a virtual team, help them prioritize their tasks and encourage them to coach one another. Performance problems can arise in teams when people get confused about what's most important and what they should be focused on. Remind your team that "instant" does not always have to mean "urgent." E-mail, overnight deliveries, and voice-mail messages don't necessarily require an immediate response. Have the team work together to prioritize tasks by their importance to the project—not according to the way a request was delivered. Agree on e-mail protocols regarding the importance of messages by marking them "high," "normal," or "low" priority and use these settings with each e-mail.

Also work to ensure that virtual team members feel that they are part of the team. In some teams, several members may work on site together, whereas other members work in isolated locations. If some team members leave a company's workspace and move to a home office, the change can be difficult for those who leave *and* for those who remain at the office. It's easy for requests made by coworkers who are physically present to take priority over requests made by virtual teammates. As the team leader and coach, you can make sure virtual teammates are still considered members of the team. How? Remind people to include all teammates in important communications. Point out virtual teammates' contributions. And encourage as much ancillary communication as possible. When feasible, hold face-to-face get-togethers.

Coming together is a beginning; keeping together
is a process; working together is success.
    —Henry Ford

Easing isolation

Isolation can be a problem when people accustomed to working in an office with colleagues suddenly find themselves spending a lot of time alone, away from the office. As the leader and coach for your team, you can help such members to obtain the social contact they need. For example, suggest more phone calls, e-mails, lunch meetings, or trips to the local office. Encourage employees, whenever possible, to look to other team members for support. If team members work from home, strongly suggest they get out of the house every day: they might have lunch with a colleague, meet associates, or visit friends. During phone conference calls, assign "break buddies" so that each remote team member receives a call during the break when everyone who is face-to-face is chatting around the coffee machine.

Addressing performance problems

Every performance problem has a source, and it's the coach's job to find it. If a team member is missing deadlines or falling behind, consider some of the following approaches:

- Contact the person and ask why. If distractions are getting in the way, find out the source of the distractions.

- Ask what you can do to help, or what changes the person might make to improve performance. For example, if the person seems overwhelmed by an assignment, work together to figure out how to break the large task into smaller tasks. Or consider assigning portions of the work to other team members who have more time.

- Identify barriers to achievement. Perhaps the team member is having difficulty working with another member of the team due to cultural differences, for example.

- Look for opportunities to help that person bond with other members of the team.

- Ensure that the team member understands and agrees to the team processes and desired outputs. At the same time, define success—what does the team member need to do to satisfy your expectations?

- Make the consequences of continued poor performance very clear. Then be sure you communicate when the team member's performance improves. With a virtual team, that may not be as easy as walking down the hall. Consider sending an e-mail or recognizing the person's achievements in a team meeting.

By nipping performance problems in the bud, you sweeten the odds that your virtual team will achieve its objectives.

Leveraging
Technology
Effectively

Technology provides the linkages through which participants in a virtual team can share ideas and information, coordinate activities, and build bonds of trust. Virtual team leaders and members don't need to be technology experts, but they must be willing and able to use or learn the technology that's required to do the job. The following guidelines can help you and your team get the most from the communication and meeting technologies now available to virtual teams.

Assessing your team's technology needs

Common sense, the team's combined knowledge, and expert help from an organization's IT department can help you find the most appropriate technology for your virtual team's purposes. Draw on those resources, but also come up with answers to the following questions:

- **Who?** Who is on the team? Are they ready to learn about and use technology? Gauging team members' attitudes toward and familiarity with technology will give you a realistic idea of what you can expect them to do with technology and how long it might take them to get up to speed.

- **What?** What does the team need to do? What is the nature of the team's work? What software does your company currently use? What compatibility issues are involved? What information do you work with now? What is the most common technology platform in the organization? What are your team's communications needs? Answering these questions will help you plan for new technology or upgrades before the team's project gets under way.

- **When?** When is your team's project scheduled to begin and end? Acquiring and installing new technology takes time, as does training people in its use. Does your overall project schedule have room for technology acquisition, installation, and training? If not, how might you gain time for these things?

- **Where?** Where will you and other team members be when you send or receive information? Where does information you need reside (in one or more databases in specific locations)? Track the desired flow of information—where it will come from and where it should go. You'll be better prepared to design an information system that suits your team's needs.

- **How?** How can you best use technology that your company and team already have? How flexible do you need to be in your use of technology? How much can you afford to spend? Analyze the possibilities of using what you have. Adapting existing technology to your needs will probably be the cheapest course to follow and may make it easier for team members to master the technology. Anticipate technology needs that may come up during the course of the project. Try to build in technology solutions today that can be adapted to your needs tomorrow.

Steps for Laying a Technology Foundation

1. **Assess time, money, and technology resources.** Schedule time and budget to lay your technology foundation. Unexpected problems and unforeseen needs can drain budgets and waste time. You don't want members of your team waiting around for software to become available, for phone lines to be installed, or for someone from IT to become available to assign passwords so they can get into the server. Setting up and running the technology end of the project can be an enormous task, requiring a high level of expertise. Assign or hire someone to assess, acquire, and maintain the technology throughout the project.

2. **Assess your existing resources.** If your organization already uses team Web sites, so much the better. Introduce as little new technology as possible. You have the basics with a team Web site and conference calls.

3. **Determine each team member's current access to technology.** What do they have? What will they need? What are they already comfortable using?

4. **Assess technology compatibility.** In the early phases of the project, particularly when team members come from different organizations with different IT systems, determine the file types that team members will exchange. Have team members send one another sample files to ensure that everyone's technology is compatible.

   - **Text documents:** If you know you will be sending documents, examine word processing software, compatibility, and compression programs.

- **Graphics and spreadsheets:** If you know you will be sending graphics or spreadsheets, look at your scanning technology, software, compression programs, and members' access to the Internet. Be sure that files can be transmitted and opened smoothly.
- **Read-only files:** If you're dealing with members who use many kinds of specialized software, consider getting everyone software that allows you to create PDF (Portable Document Format) or other read-only files. Graphics, spreadsheets, flow charts, and other documents can be transformed to a universal, read-only format for review and distribution. Only the people who work on the files directly need to have the actual software that creates them.
- **Phone and videoconferencing:** If your team needs to engage in frequent brainstorming sessions, check out options *before* you need to use them. Test your equipment to see whether it's doing the job and to evaluate whether you need more speakerphones, Web cams, and/or headsets.

"Steps for Laying a Technology Foundation" provides additional guidance for this aspect of leading your virtual team.

Establishing rules about e-mail

Everyone on a virtual team needs—at the very minimum—an e-mail address that they can access from anywhere. If you plan to rely heavily on e-mailing attached documents, check for compatibility and compression issues with each team member. Try to avoid this, however, and instead encourage the team to agree to post all documents to the team Web site.

Also establish protocols for use—everyone on the team should know when to send e-mails, why, and to whom. Be clear about who must be copied on what. Don't overdo it. There's no need to copy every person on the team list on every e-mail. Nobody wants to receive massive amounts of irrelevant e-mail. But don't underdo it, either. Make sure everyone is informed about decisions that affect them, and that people who need to be in on decisions are consulted. E-mails can help create virtual paper trails and can be important documents down the line if misunderstandings or conflicts arise. Better than e-mail, however, is the use of discussion capabilities on team Web sites. They're more transparent and less time-consuming for people to review than individual e-mails.

"Tips for Writing an E-Mail Message" offers additional advice about this aspect of virtual-team communication.

Using Web sites and intranet sites

The Web has changed the way virtual teams can work. A team Web site can substitute for the old team "war room"— the physical space where members of same-place teams gather to discuss ideas, socialize, and get updates on the project. Via their browsers, virtual team members can go to a team Web site where they can find everything they need to do their work—the mission, goals, tasks, and deliverables; who's involved with what aspect of the project; how to contact one another; schedules; and any other related information. Most companies have some version of this

Tips for Writing an E-Mail Message

- Send a separate e-mail for each topic. That makes it easier for recipients to respond to and file or delete the message.
- Use the subject line to make a clear statement or specific request. This will make your message stand out in a recipient's crowded inbox.
- Put the most important content at the beginning; recipients don't always scroll down to the end.
- Make it brief, focused, specific. Deliver the most information in the least space.
- Keep paragraphs short (three or four lines). Attach files if you need to send something longer or you need to use headings, bullets, tables, graphics, and other formats that make your message easier to read and understand. But avoid attachments when you can post the same information to the team Web site.
- When replying, include a copy of the original text. This is a handy reminder for recipients who might not recall what they wrote previously.
- Never write e-mail when your emotions are raging. Anger and sarcasm often come across more strongly in text than they would in a face-to-face communication. An e-mail is a permanent record that can come back to haunt you.
- Don't use all capital letters because it looks like you're shouting.
- Don't use inappropriate humor.
- Proofread! Always review your message before pressing Send. Think "AAAA," double checking that your message contains:

a correct *address,* correct *attached* files, suitable *attitude* and
tone, and a statement of the *action* you want the recipient
to take.

---

operating now; if yours doesn't, inexpensive Web services are now
available.

A virtual team room can be set up in the project Web site using
"walls," like those in a real team room. In the virtual world, however, you're not limited to four walls:

- **Purpose wall:** This wall includes the team charter, goals,
  tasks, a list of deliverables, and current results.

- **People wall:** This section identifies the team members and
  states their roles. Here, members can find out who is involved with which aspect of the project. If possible, include a
  photo of each team member and a brief description of his or
  her particular work and expertise. Putting a face and a bit of
  history with a name adds an important dimension to virtual
  teamwork.

- **Meeting wall:** This part of the site contains a schedule of
  upcoming meetings and their agendas. Minutes of past
  meetings and any meeting presentations are also stored on
  this wall. Members can use this wall to post their work for
  review by colleagues. Those reviews and comments can likewise be posted.

- **Communication/Links wall:** This section contains links to information the team needs. For example, it might offer a link

to research reports or other studies that the team needs to do its work. It might also contain a list of the team's operating agreements for e-mailing, phone calling, and other routine team communications.

- **Time wall:** This area of the team site contains everything related to schedules, progress, Gantt charts, holiday and vacation schedules, and timely messages.

- **Content wall:** This is where all the team's working documents go. Everything the team produces goes in this area.

Web sites are valuable assets, but they require tending. Someone must monitor and update the site, as well as fix any technical problems that arise. Depending on the scope of the project, this could be a full-time job for a team member. Make sure that you consider the technical needs associated with a team Web site before the project gets under way.

"Tips for Establishing a Team Web Site" provides additional ideas.

Using databases, fax machines, and group document software

Databases contain documents and other information that's useful to the team. They are accessible from Web sites and intranet sites. Documents (often called records) in databases often contain sensitive material. Some virtual team members may be allowed to change such documents, but your organization may want to restrict that capability. For example, team members who are not

Tips for Establishing a Team Web Site

- Employ a team Web site that is flexible enough to accommodate growth, change, and use on more than one project.
- Ensure that the site is comprehensive enough to grow without becoming cumbersome.
- Guarantee that the site follows a logical, intuitive format for uploading and downloading information.
- Make sure the site lets you customize a unique graphic look and feel that will give your team an identity.
- Confirm that the site is up and running *before* the project starts. Introduce and demonstrate the site at the launch meeting.
- Designate someone to oversee management of the site throughout the project.

employed by your company (such as customers or vendors) may have access to view restricted documents but may not be able to edit them.

The dedicated *fax machine* is on its way out as a mode of communication. Many of its functions can be done more easily by posting to the team Web site or, if necessary, through attachments to e-mail. Even documents, newspaper clippings, photos, and so forth can be posted or sent as e-mail attachments if they are scanned into files. But many people do not have easy access to scanners, and scanning can take time. Thus, fax machines can continue to serve a useful purpose for some virtual teams when more modern technology is not available.

Group document software can also be useful. Teams are forever generating and submitting reports. Because several members might collaborate in report development, they need a handy way of incorporating changes into electronic files. Chances are, the word processors used in your organization have a feature that allows users to track changes made in a document. But some members of your team may not be aware of this feature. Others may be aware of it but may not have any experience in using it. Tech-savvy organizations use Web-based group editing software. Check with your IT department to see what it has available.

Using live-meeting technology

There are times when e-mails won't do—when team members simply must get together to talk about their work. In other words, they need a "live" meeting. For the most part, phone conferencing serves the live meeting function for the virtual team. For example, a team member wants to speak directly with a customer about how he has adapted the team's product to make it more effective.

In other cases, people may need to see each other. This is especially important when new people have just joined the team and others need to get to know them. Or perhaps team members need to see the physical objects that others are working on: a product prototype, or different color choices for a new package design. Although face-to-face is not always possible, it's beneficial when it does happen.

Here are some ways to bring virtual teams together for "live" meetings:

- **Telephone conferencing:** The telephone conference is the quickest and easiest way for the virtual team to

Steps for Maintaining Version Control of Documents

1. **Choose software that makes it easy.** Your company's IT department may be able to offer suggestions on this.

2. **Determine naming conventions.** Before getting under way, establish naming conventions for files, folders, and dates. File names should be easily understandable. Post the conventions wherever people will be sure to see them: as part of the team's operating agreements, on the intranet, on a mousepad—whatever it takes so that people pay attention to them.

3. **Decide who owns what files.** Several people may work on one file, but maintaining the file should be one person's ultimate responsibility.

4. **Clarify procedures for archiving files.** When a new version of a file is created, the old file should be archived. Work with team members to develop a good way to archive files. Archives should be easily accessible during the life of the project and always stored in the same place on the team Web site.

communicate verbally. A telephone conference is often necessary to review key deliverables, discuss strategy, and brainstorm. Many kinds of phone-conference technologies exist, from built-in conferencing in telephone systems to conferences hosted by communication service providers—and nearly every company has these available. "Tips for Making Conference Calls" offers additional ideas for using this technology.

Tips for Making Conference Calls

- Create an agenda for the conference call. Distribute the agenda and any other documents relevant to the meeting before the conference call takes place.

- Make sure that the speakers at every end of the call can be heard. (If you experience technical difficulty with your in-house conferencing system, consider using the conference call services of a telephone provider that acts as host.)

- Always use webconferencing so that everyone is looking at the same information. This also prevents multitasking and people's attention wandering.

- Assign one person as facilitator to keep the agenda moving, another as note taker so that meeting notes go out promptly, and a third person to keep an eye on the time.

- Place each person at a different "hour" on the face of an imaginary clock. When you jump into the conversation, preface your statement with "This is [your name] at six o'clock." This helps people get used to one another's voices. Some teams put together a graphic of the clock with everyone's pictures on it and post it to their team Web site.

- Speak clearly—don't shout (especially on a speakerphone), and avoid slang that may not be familiar to call participants from other regions, cultures, or countries.

- Pose questions to individuals who are not engaged in the discussion in order to draw them into the discussion.

- Limit interruptions and digressions.

- Avoid letting one person dominate the conversation.

- Don't try to do anything else while on the call. If you must attend to something else briefly, use your Mute button or put the call on hold.

- Avoid status reporting on calls, and use the precious real time to brainstorm, resolve differences, and make decisions. Team members can read the status reports before the meeting.

- Conclude the call as you would any meeting, making sure that everyone "checks out," just as they would when leaving a face-to-face meeting. As team leader, you can summarize what was said, confirm decisions, and reiterate steps for future action.

- Distribute notes of the meeting as soon as possible by posting them to the team Web site, and follow up on action steps immediately.

- **Videoconferencing:** Videoconferencing is another channel that can encourage team connectivity. It can serve the purpose of bringing teams together without spending time or money on meals, travel, and lodging. Team members located in London, for example, can see and interact with their colleagues in Rome without leaving their offices. However, videoconferencing can be complicated and costly, only a limited number can participate meaningfully, and it typically requires the help of people with technical skills. For basic video, each participant needs the appropriate computer, camera, microphone, software, and Internet connection. Unfortunately, systems from different vendors aren't always compatible with different computers. So if your team opts for video, be sure everyone gets a compatible system.

- **Webconferencing:** By logging into the same Web site, using shared screen technology, everyone on the team can look at the same information in the same way. People can share documents on their local computers and can pass control from team member to team member. For instance, if a team leader in Houston, Texas, wants to share a presentation, control shifts to that person. Then, if someone in London wants to draw a diagram using the electronic whiteboard function available in some software, control passes to that person, and the rest of the team will be able to see the image take shape on their computer screens. This makes it possible for team members to discuss the sketch and recommend changes—all in real time.

Tips and Tools

Tools for Leading
Virtual Teams

Contact Information Form for Virtual Team Members

Use this form to record each team member's contact information, including how and when he or she prefers to be reached. Remember to reference the time zones of global team members. Include country codes in phone numbers. Post this to your project Web site, or e-mail it as an attachment to all team members.

TEAM MEMBER			
Role		Address	
E-mail			
Work phone		Time zone	
Mobile phone		Best time to call	
Fax		Preferred form of correspondence	

TEAM MEMBER			
Role		Address	
E-mail			
Work phone		Time zone	
Mobile phone		Best time to call	
Fax		Preferred form of correspondence	

TEAM MEMBER			
Role		Address	
E-mail			
Work phone		Time zone	
Mobile phone		Best time to call	
Fax		Preferred form of correspondence	

TEAM MEMBER			
Role		Address	
E-mail			
Work phone		Time zone	
Mobile phone		Best time to call	
Fax		Preferred form of correspondence	

Setting Up a Virtual Team

Use this worksheet to establish a strong foundation for a virtual team.

What is the vision for the team?

What are the team's goals?

What roles will each team member play?

What will be each team member's responsibilities?

What kinds of decisions will the team have the authority to make?

Who will make what types of decisions?

What, precisely, is the team expected to deliver?

When is the team's work expected to be finished?

How will the team's success be measured?

What are the major milestones the team will reach while progressing toward its goal?

What are the major risks associated with the team's goals, and how will those risks be addressed?

How will commitment to the team be sustained throughout the project?

How will leadership be shared among team members?

Identifying Roles and Responsibilities

Use this form to clarify roles and responsibilities of virtual team members. Post this form on your project Web site or e-mail a copy as an attachment to all members.

Posted by: E-mail: Phone:

Team Member	Role (title)	Key Responsibilities	Location

Culture Check

Use this worksheet to perform a "culture check" to address the special challenges that arise in virtual teams.

Working Conditions

How much will team members be expected to travel?

What resources will be available to them for getting their work done?

Hours of Operation

How many hours per day or week are team members expected to work on this project?

How early or late are team members expected to be available for phone or videoconferences?

Authority and Delegation

Who will be responsible for making what types of decisions as the team does its work?

Who has the authority to assign work to specific team members?

Communication Patterns

What are team members' assumptions about appropriate and acceptable communication—in particular, what is considered polite or impolite communication?

Virtual Team Work Plan

Use this form to detail the tasks that team members need to accomplish according to schedule. This can be posted to a project Web site or circulated as an e-mail attachment. It is designed to be updated frequently.

Keeper of plan: Date of plan update:

Goal 1:

Tasks	Member(s) Responsible	Target Date	Results/Task Completion Date	Reviewed/ Approval Date

Goal 2:

Tasks	Member(s) Responsible	Target Date	Results/Task Completion Date	Reviewed/ Approval Date

Test Yourself

This section offers ten multiple-choice questions to help you identify your baseline knowledge of the essentials of leading virtual teams.

Answers to the questions are given at the end of the test.

1. Virtual teams have become common in business today. Which of the following statements best describes a virtual team?

  a. A virtual team makes it easier for a company to bring together a group of people who have similar skills, experiences, and knowledge about customers and business.

  b. A virtual team typically consists of some members who are linked through communication that is not face-to-face.

  c. A virtual team enables a company to establish a standardized workday based on the operating hours of the company that has created the team.

2. On virtual teams, the chances of things going awry are much greater than on same-place teams. How can you, as the leader of a virtual team, best build a strong foundation for success?

  a. Select members for your team who have a strong natural interest in the team's goals, as well as the skills required to do the job.

b. Retain a firm grip on leadership of your team to ensure that projects proceed as planned and everyone remains focused on the goal.

c. Set hours of operation based on the geographic area in which most of the team members are working, so that few members will have to work during evenings.

3. You're leading a virtual team and want to do your best to foster team identity. Which of the following practices would you apply?

a. Avoid arranging face-to-face meetings at important project junctures unless the entire team can come together.

b. Encourage team members to contact you whenever they have concerns about the project; you'll send the message that support is always available.

c. Establish subgroups at a launch meeting and charge them with discussing specific facets of the team's project.

4. You know that open lines of communication are essential to building mutual trust in your virtual team. Which of the following steps would you take to establish good communication?

a. Hold a meeting after the project has been completed to review what went well and what could be improved upon for future virtual team projects.

b. Create a team roster before the team begins its work.

c. Halfway through the project, review the team's goals and ways of measuring progress.

5. You know that coaching can help ensure that every member of your team gets the help he or she needs to solve problems and improve performance. Which steps would you take to ensure that coaching is available to your team members?

    a. Remind team members to respond as quickly as possible to e-mail and voice-mail messages, so problems can be addressed promptly.

    b. Encourage team members to help one another identify and solve problems related to accomplishing their assigned tasks.

    c. Allow team members to initiate conversations with you about problems they've been having, then suggest ways of helping them.

6. You want your virtual team to get the best results from technology. Which of the following approaches would best help you?

    a. Avoid using existing technology; it probably will not be customized sufficiently for your team's needs.

    b. Select technology only after the team's project is under way, so you can determine compatibility and other issues based on actual experience.

    c. Ask whether the team's project schedule has room for technology acquisition, installation, and training.

7. Your virtual team is up and running, and you want to ensure that people make the best possible use of e-mail technology. What do you do?

a. Check for compatibility and file compression issues with each member of your team.

b. Advise team members to copy all other members on any e-mail communications, to foster information flow and adequate communication.

c. Provide e-mail addresses only for those team members who need them, to avoid e-mailing overload.

8. You're establishing a team Web site for your virtual team. What is the *first* thing you should consider as you set up the site?

a. The need to post the team's charter, goals, and tasks.

b. The need to find someone to monitor and update the site, as well as fix any technical problems.

c. The need to create a virtual team room on the project Web site by setting up "walls" to manage the team's purpose, people, content, meetings, schedules, and communication.

9. The members of your team need to explore new product designs and suggest and see recommended changes implemented in real time. Which live-meeting technology would you select to enable them to accomplish these tasks?

a. Videoconferencing.

b. Webconferencing with an electronic whiteboard.

10. You're conducting a "culture check" for your virtual team and want to make sure that the team establishes useful processes for working together. What do you do?

a. Encourage team members to share decision making with people from their own region who report to them.

b. Explain to team members the amount of travel you expect them to handle in order to achieve the team's goals.

c. Collectively decide who has the authority to assign work to specific team members.

Answers to test questions

1, b. The term *virtual team* refers to a team that, for the most part, is linked through communication that is not face-to-face. For example, the team may be linked through e-mail, voice mail, telephone conferencing, videoconferencing, and Internet-based forums. Some teams are entirely virtual; their members rarely, if ever, meet face-to-face. Other teams are partially virtual; they include some members who work together in an office as well as other company employees in global locations, or representatives of a key supplier in a different country, or perhaps important customers from all over the world.

2, a. Selecting people who have an interest in the team's goals is a good way to build commitment to the team and its objectives. Commitment is crucial for ensuring that team members allocate their energy and time to the team, not to other demands that may seem more pressing because they have a more immediate, physical presence.

3, c. It's helpful to establish these subgroups at a one- or two-day launch meeting for the team. Subgroups can help build small-group cohesion, which encourages collaboration and helps people to get to know one another on a professional and personal level. By rotating through subgroups, everyone has a chance to meet and work with everyone else on the team.

4, b. A team roster lists all team members, their role on the team, the best way to contact them, their location and time zone, and the hours during which they will be available for participating in phone conferences or videoconferences and responding to e-mails. When combined with other documents and agreements about team goals and processes, the roster communicates expectations about how the team will work together.

5, b. Part of coaching a virtual team is leveraging your team members' broad range of skills and knowledge. Be sure all members are familiar with one another's unique abilities and knowledge—such as preparing budget reports, using a particular software application, or resolving interpersonal conflicts. Encourage members to call on one another for coaching assistance if needed.

6, c. Acquiring and installing new technology takes time, as does training people in its use. By asking whether your team's project schedule has room for these activities, you can identify shortfalls and find ways to gain time for these activities.

7, a. If you plan to rely heavily on e-mailing attached documents, you'll need to ensure that team members can open one another's compressed files as well as open and read attached files created using different software programs. Checking for compatibility and compression issues ahead of time can help you anticipate and address any problems.

8, b. Virtual team Web sites are valuable assets, but they require tending. Someone must "own" this responsibility. Depending on the scope of the project, this could be a full-time job for a team member.

9, b. With webconferencing that has an electronic whiteboard, team members can share documents, diagrams, and other information, as well as see a drawing or chart on their laptops as the document is being created. If members are also connected by telephone, they can discuss the sketch and recommend changes in real time.

10, c. By establishing the conditions for authority and delegation, you prevent misunderstandings that might occur later as team members begin working together. In a virtual team, members share leadership—thus it's not always the team leader who delegates tasks.

To Learn More

Articles

Apgar, Mahlon, IV. "The Alternative Workplace: Changing Where and How People Work." *Harvard Business Review* OnPoint Enhanced Edition. Boston: Harvard Business School Publishing, 2000.

Although estimates vary widely, it is safe to say that some 30 to 40 million people in the United States are now either telecommuters or home-based workers. What motivates managers to examine how people spend their time at the office and where else they might do their work? Among the potential benefits for companies are reduced costs, increased productivity, and an edge in vying for and keeping talented employees. They can also capture government incentives and avoid costly sanctions. But at the same time, alternative workplace programs are not for everyone. Indeed, such programs can be difficult to adopt, even for those organizations that seem to be most suited to them. Ingrained behaviors and practical hurdles are hard to overcome. And the challenges of managing both the cultural changes and systems improvements required by an alternative workplace initiative are substantial.

Handy, Charles. "Trust and the Virtual Organization." *Harvard Business Review* OnPoint Enhanced Edition. Boston: Harvard Business School Publishing, 2000.

The technological possibilities of the virtual organization are seductive. But its managerial and personal implications require rethinking old notions of control. As it becomes possible for more work to be done outside the traditional office, trust will become more important to organizations. Handy proposes seven rules of trust: (1) *trust is not blind*—it needs fairly small groupings in which people can know each other well; (2) *trust needs boundaries*—define a goal, and then leave the worker to get on with it; (3) *trust demands learning and openness to change*; (4) *trust is tough*—when it turns out to be misplaced, people have to go; (5) *trust needs bonding*—the goals of small units must gel with the larger group's; (6) *trust needs touch*—workers must sometimes meet in person; (7) *trust requires leaders*. According to Handy, virtuality's Three I's (information, ideas, intelligence) can improve quality of life, but he also asks the question, Will they be for everyone? He believes the potential exists for the Three I's to benefit not just organizations but also those with whom they do business and society as a whole.

Harvard Business School Publishing. "Communicating with Virtual Project Teams." *Harvard Management Communication Letter,* December 2000.

How do you bring a project team together when its members are spread over several continents and time zones? Enter a new breed of Internet-based products called "virtual workspaces."

These products offer a password-protected site, with services ranging from e-mail and information storage to chat rooms and scheduling. This article describes some of the pros and cons of such services and lists Web site addresses to help you learn more about the services.

Harvard Business School Publishing. "Creating Successful Virtual Organizations." *Harvard Management Communication Letter,* December 2000.

In many ways, the world of work is entirely different from what it was just a decade ago. You work with people you never see—and may have never even met. Your colleagues come and go at all hours and in all manner of dress, and they may not even be actual employees of the same company. This complexity adds up to one thing: good communication is more difficult—and more necessary—than ever. This article turns to the experts for some ground rules on communication in the virtual age.

Majchrzak, Ann, Arvind Malhotra, Jeffrey Stamps, and Jessica Lipnack. "Can Absence Make a Team Grow Stronger?" *Harvard Business Review,* May 2004.

Remarkably, an extensive benchmarking study reveals that it isn't necessary to bring team members together to get their best work. The scores of successful virtual teams the authors examined didn't have many of the psychological and practical obstacles that plagued their more traditional, face-to-face counterparts. Team members felt freer to contribute—especially outside their established areas of expertise. Rather than depend on videoconferencing or e-mail, successful virtual teams made extensive use of sophisticated online team rooms. Differences were most effectively hashed out in teleconferences, which team leaders also used to foster group identity and solidarity.

Ross, Judith A. "Trust Makes the Team Go 'Round." *Harvard Management Update,* June 2006.

As many highly accomplished managers are discovering, managing virtually is not the same as managing face-to-face. Cultural and language differences become magnified, as do conflicts. It is much easier to hide errors and problems, sweep misunderstandings under the rug, and make erroneous assumptions. And such mistakes and mix-ups are more likely to become full-fledged disasters when the group does not feel free to acknowledge and address them openly. Don't panic. These problems are not inevitable—as long as team leaders remember to focus on one critical element as they build and manage their virtual operations: trust. Expanding on a November 2005 study by The Conference Board, *Harvard Management Update* polled a number of experts and practitioners and compiled a list of six steps to boost trust in dispersed operations and virtual teams.

Books

Duarte, Deborah L. and Nancy Tennant Snyder. *Mastering Virtual Teams: Strategies, Tools, and Techniques That Succeed.* San Francisco: Jossey-Bass, 1999.

Designed for people who lead or work with virtual teams, this guide is divided into sections that cover starting a team and keeping it in operation. The authors draw upon their experience in academic and business environments, and provide real-world examples as well as many useful checklists and practical exercises.

Fisher, Kimball and Mareen Duncan Fisher. *The Distance Manager: A Hands-on Guide to Managing Off-Site Employees and Virtual Teams.* New York: McGraw-Hill, 2001.

The Distance Manager teaches managers the skills needed to manage off-site employees and virtual teams, including how to motivate and inspire employees, how to coach for peak performance, how to build a cohesive team composed of workers in different locations, how to lead people who are not subordinates, and more.

Lipnack, Jessica and Jeffrey Stamps. *Virtual Teams: People Working Across Boundaries with Technology.* New York: John Wiley & Sons, 2000.

Leading experts in networked organizations show you how to effectively start, implement, and maintain virtual teams in your organization. The authors present the 90/10 rule, which stresses how a virtual team's success is based 90% on the people involved and 10% on the technology.

eLearning Programs

Harvard Business School Publishing. *Managing Virtual Teams.* Boston: Harvard Business School Publishing, 2000.

This program will prepare you to successfully work with and lead a virtual team. You will learn about the four factors that make up an efficient and effective virtual team:

- Great people

- Effective communication

- Appropriate technology

- A shared vision and process

Through interactive role play, expert guidance, and activities for immediate application at work, this workshop will help you understand and improve your ability to work and communicate through virtual channels. Pre- and post-assessments and additional resources complete the workshop, preparing you to lead a virtual team.

Sources for Leading Virtual Teams

The following sources aided in development of this book:

Crandall, N. Fredric and Marc J. Wallace, Jr. *Work and Rewards in the Virtual Workplace: A New Deal for Organizations and Employees.* New York: AMACOM, American Management Association, 1998.

Goldsmith, George and Cory LeFebvre. *Virtual Work: Real Results.* The Interactive Manager Series. Interactive multimedia CD-ROM. Boston: Harvard Business School Publishing, 1998.

Harvard Business School Publishing. *Creating Teams with an Edge.* Boston: Harvard Business School Press, 2004.

Lipnack, Jessica and Jeffrey Stamps. *Virtual Teams: Reaching Across Space, Time, and Organizations with Technology.* New York: John Wiley & Sons, 2000.

Notes

Notes

Notes

How to Order Page

Harvard Business School Press publications are available world-wide from your local bookseller or online retailer.

You can also call:
1-800-668-6780

Our product consultants are available to help you 8:00 a.m.–6:00 p.m., Monday–Friday, Eastern Time. Outside the U.S. and Canada, call: 617-783-7450.

Please call about special discounts for quantities greater than ten.

You can order online at:
www.HBSPress.org